In this beautifully illustrated book, you'll discover and learn about 20 inspiring Black figures (bo   women) from History.

The stories start from as far back as the 1   which was more than 700 years ago!

We'll move through each Century, learning all about the people who helped build and create the wonderful world we live in today.

From Mansa Musa, to Harriet Tubman, & Muhammed Ali - there's something for everyone to discover and be amazed by.

And, we've hand-illustrated each famous figure, so you can picture exactly how they looked!

So, let's begin by looking back at the first Black Icon!

Mansa Musa

The Richest Man in All of History

Mansa Musa is not a well-known historical figure, but what we do know is that he was actually the richest man in all of history!

Yes, that means he was richer than Elon Musk, richer than Jeff Bezos, and richer than anybody else alive today!

The African King, born in 1280, is most remembered for his journey to Mecca, giving out bars of gold to everybody he encountered. On this journey, he was supported by more than 60,000 men, all wearing the finest Persian silk. They gave away so much Gold in Cairo, Egypt, that the price of gold crashed and stayed low for 10 years.

We should be inspired by Mansa Musa because, by knowing the richest man in the world was Black, we know there is nothing stopping us from attaining as much money as we want in today's age. He was also extremely generous, something that we should all strive for.

If you'd like to learn more about Mansa Musa, you can watch documentaries on YouTube. History is full of fascinating stories, and he's one of them!

Nyatsimba Mutota

A Brave Warrior Prince

There lived a brave warrior named Nyatsimba Mutota in a faraway place called Great Zimbabwe. Let's travel back to 1430 to learn about his incredible journey.

His adventurous spirit led him on a quest to the north in search of a precious resource - salt! Along his journey, he encountered the Shona-Tavara, but it wasn't just salt that he found. With unwavering courage, he led his army to victory over the Tonga and Tavara tribes. This victorious path ultimately led him to establish his own dynasty atop the majestic Chitakochangonya Hill, and it became the famous Kingdom of Mutapa.

What can we learn from Nyatsimba Mutota? Well, he shows us how important it is to be brave and never give up, even when things are tough. Nyatsimba's story inspires us to be bold, dream big dreams, and work together to overcome challenges.

If you want to discover more about Nyatsimba Mutota, you can read books about African history or read "Prince Mutota and Friends: A Great Zimbabwe Adventure." Remember, learning about amazing people like Nyatsimba Mutota can help us understand the past and inspire us to do great things in the future.

Yasuke was a brave and extraordinary person who lived long ago in Japan. He was a samurai, just like the heroes you see in your favorite cartoons and books! But what makes Yasuke really special is that he was a Black samurai, and he did some incredible things!

He became a samurai in Japan, even though he came from a different country. He was so strong and skilled with a sword that he caught the eye of a powerful leader named Oda Nobunaga. Yasuke became Nobunaga's loyal samurai, and they went on exciting adventures together.

In 1582, during a big battle, he survived a terrible ambush but lost his friend Nobunaga. After that, Yasuke's life became a mystery. What he did next remains unknown, making Yasuke's story even more intriguing.

From Yasuke, we learn that no matter where you're from or what you look like, if you work hard and believe in yourself, you can achieve great things. He reminds us to be brave and to always stand up for what we believe in, just like a true samurai.

You can learn even more about Yasuke by reading books like "African Samurai: The True Story of Yasuke, a Legendary Black Warrior in Feudal Japan," or watching videos about his incredible journey. Many exciting stories and adventures are waiting for you to explore, just like Yasuke did in ancient Japan!

Nzinga Mbandi

The Warrior Queen Of Africa

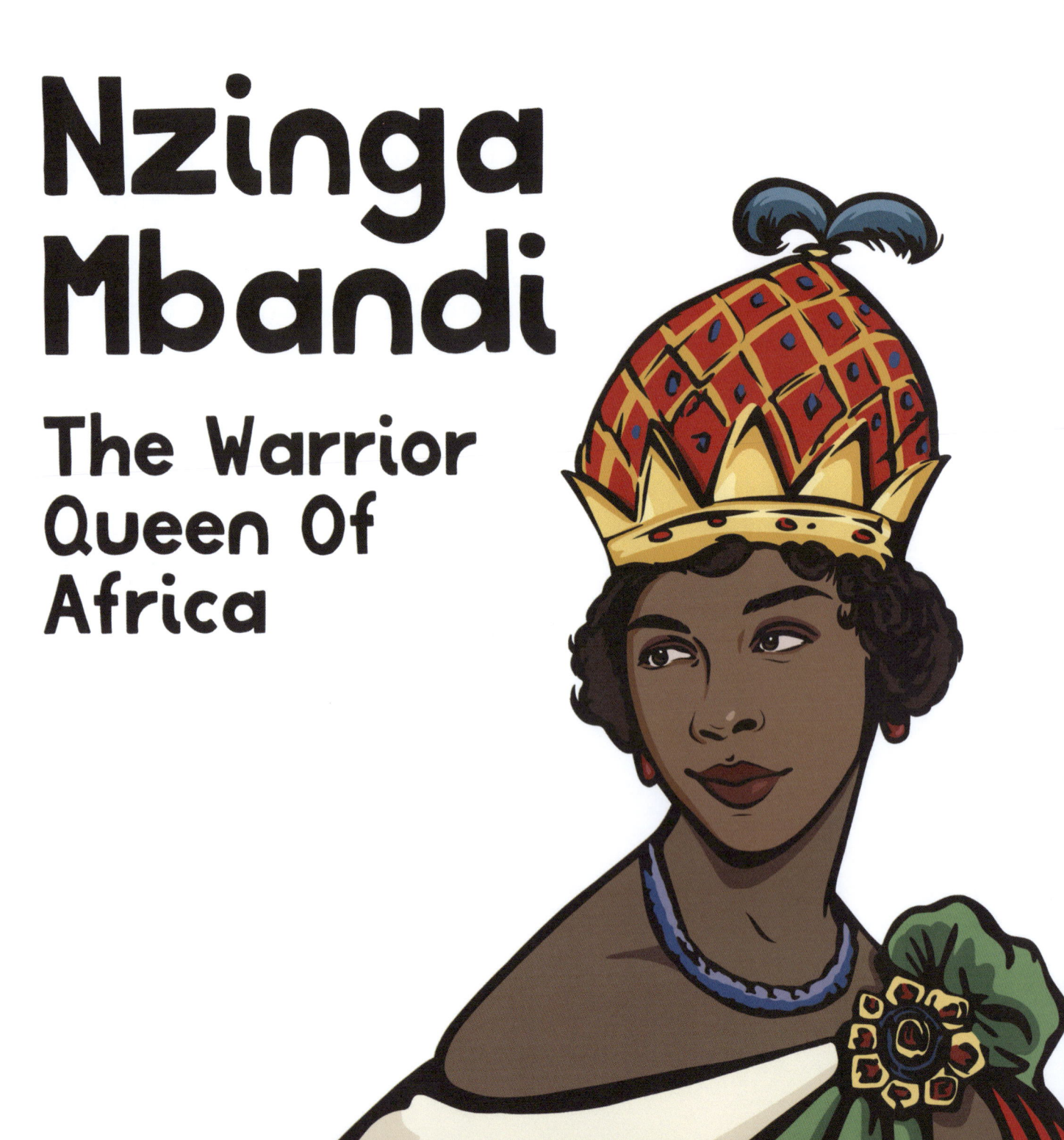

Nzinga Mbandi, a fearless warrior queen, skilled negotiator, and outstanding military general, lived in the 17th century in a land called Angola in Central Africa. She was a remarkable leader who did many brave things.

Queen Nzinga ruled over two kingdoms, Ndongo and Matamba, and she protected her people from the Portuguese and their slave trade. She never gave up, even when things were tough. She used her cleverness to make agreements with other leaders and fought in battles to defend her kingdoms.

Queen Nzinga shows us that we can stand up for what is right no matter how young or old we are. She reminds us that being clever and brave can make a big difference. We should never stop trying, even when things are difficult. Nzinga Mbandi's determination and courage are inspiring!

To learn more about this incredible queen, you can read "Njinga of Angola: Africa's Warrior Queen." You can also explore videos on YouTube that have information about African history. Queen Nzinga's story is one of strength and bravery everyone should know about.

Remember, Queen Nzinga Mbandi was a true hero who showed us that we can make a positive impact on the world if we are determined and courageous.

Abram Gannibal

A Remarkable Russian Hero

Meet Abram Petrovich Gannibal – a truly extraordinary person from long ago. He lived in Russia, and his life story is like an exciting adventure!

Abram Gannibal wasn't just any person; he became a brilliant military engineer and even a general-in-chief in Russia. But what makes his story even more amazing is how he got there. When he was just a little kid, he was kidnapped and made a slave by the Ottomans. However, his life took a surprising turn when he was given as a gift to Peter the Great, the famous Russian Emperor. Peter the Great not only set him free but also adopted him as his own godson. Gannibal grew up in the Emperor's court, and his intelligence and hard work made him a great military leader!

Abram Gannibal's story teaches us about strength and resilience. Even when things seemed really tough, he never gave up. He used his brain and his talents to become an important person in Russia. His determination inspires us and reminds us that no matter where we come from, we can achieve amazing things with hard work and courage.

To learn more about Abram Petrovich Gannibal, you can read "The Stolen Prince" by Hugh Barnes or watch videos on YouTube about him to discover about the incredible adventures of this African hero who became a Russian general. His story will surely make you feel proud and inspired!

Phillis Wheatley
The African Genius

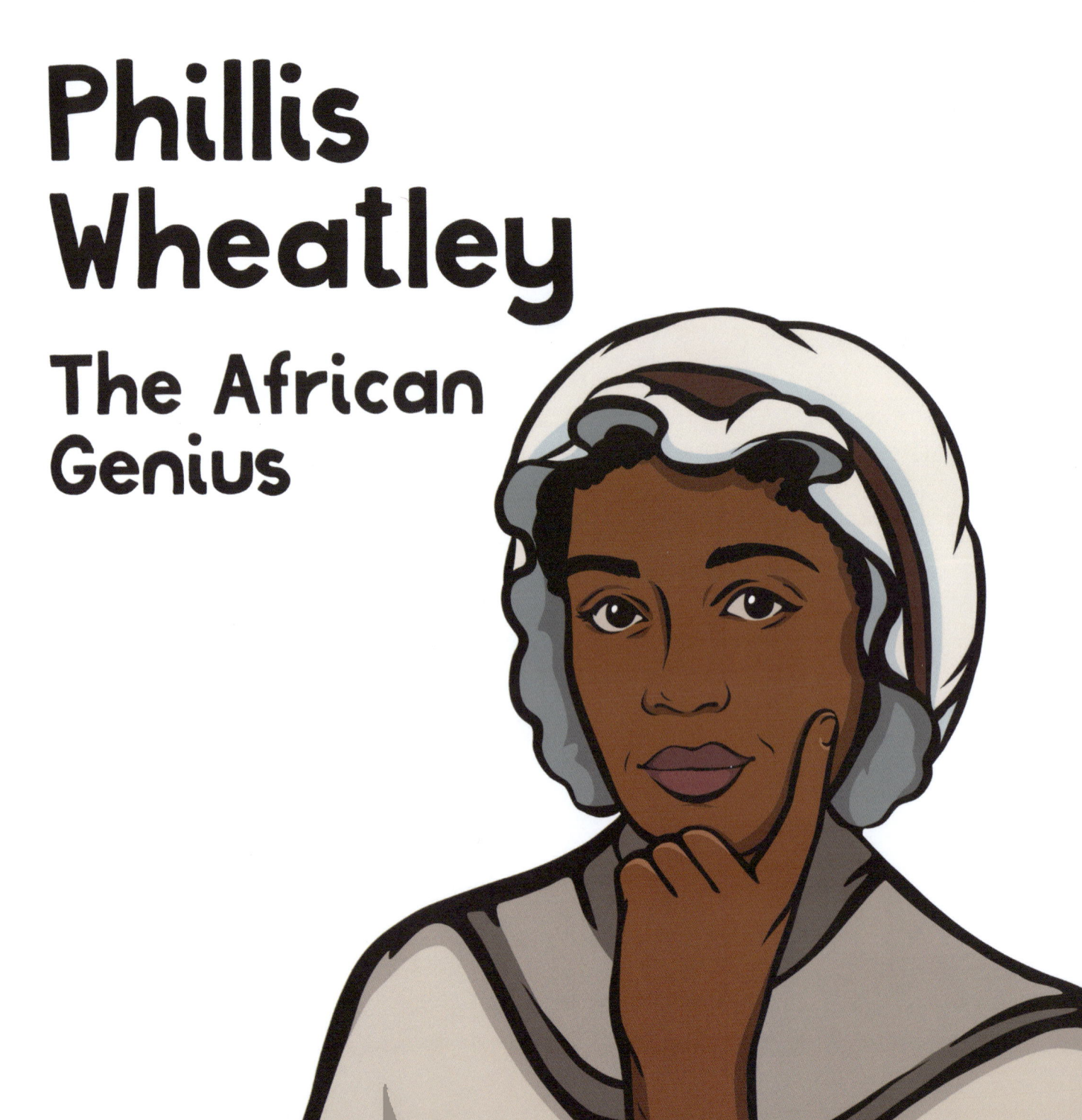

Phillis Wheatley Peters lived long ago, in the 18th century, when America was just beginning to grow as a country. She was born in Africa but came to America as an enslaved person. However, she did something amazing – she became one of the best-known poets of her time!

Even though Phillis was enslaved, she was lucky to be educated in the home of a kind man named John Wheatley in Boston. She wrote beautiful poems that were published in books. People in both America and England loved her poems, and they thought she was incredibly smart and talented. She even got to meet important leaders in America and England!

Phillis Wheatley teaches us that we can still achieve amazing things with our talents and hard work, no matter where we come from or what challenges we face. She was a shining example of how people can be both artistic (like writing poems) and intellectual (being very smart). Her poems also helped inspire people to fight against slavery and believe in equality for all.

If you want to learn more about Phillis Wheatley, you can read some of her beautiful poems, like "Poems of Phillis Wheatley" or "Being Brought from Africa to America." They are like windows into her thoughts and feelings. You can also visit a library or look up more information online to explore her incredible life story.

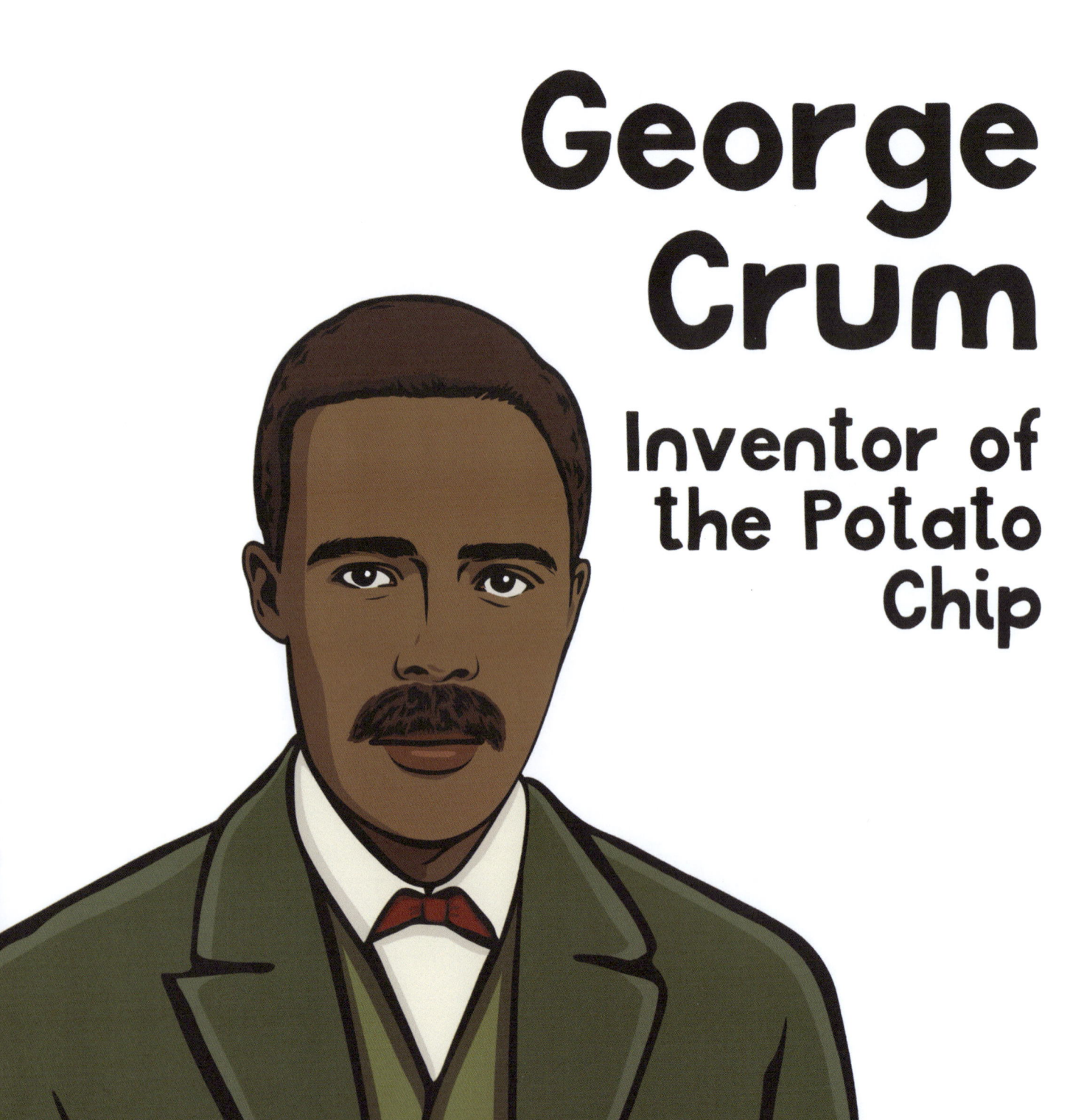

During the mid-1800s, in a place called Saratoga Springs, there was a clever chef named George Crum. He worked in a restaurant called Moon's Lake House, where he cooked delicious food.

George Crum is famous for inventing something super yummy - potato chips! But here's the funny part: It all started because of a picky customer. This customer kept sending back his French fries, saying they were too thick. George Crum wanted to teach him a lesson, so he sliced some potatoes super-duper thin, fried them until they were crispy, and sprinkled lots of salt on top. And guess what? The customer loved it! That's how potato chips were born.

We can learn that sometimes, when life gives you challenges (or picky customers), you can turn them into something amazing! George Crum didn't get mad; he got creative. He showed us that even when things don't go as planned, we can come up with cool ideas and surprise ourselves.

If you want to learn more about George Crum, you can read "George Crum and the Saratoga Chip" by Gaylia Taylor. His potato chip story is a tasty piece of history!

So, remember, even when life gets a little tricky, you can be as creative as George Crum and make something wonderful. Who knows, you might invent the next yummy snack!

Harriet Tubman

The Moses of Her People

Long, long ago in the United States, there lived an amazing woman named Harriet Tubman. She did something so incredible that people called her the "Moses of her people."

Harriet Tubman was once enslaved, which means she didn't have the freedom to do what she wanted. But she was really smart and brave. She managed to escape and then helped lots of others escape, too! She was like a superhero, guiding them to freedom on the "Underground Railroad," a secret network of safe houses and routes that helped enslaved people escape to freedom. During a big war called the Civil War, she also worked as a spy, a soldier, and even a nurse. Imagine that! She was the very first African-American woman to do all these amazing things!

Harriet Tubman teaches us that no matter how tough things may seem, we should never give up on our dreams and help others. She was strong, kind, and never stopped fighting for what she believed in. Her bravery and kindness can inspire us to make the world a better place.

If you want to learn more about this incredible hero, you can read "Harriet Tubman: The Road to Freedom" by Catherine Clinton or watch the movie "Harriet." She's a real-life hero, and her story is full of amazing adventures!

Rebecca Lee Crumpler

America's First Black Female Doctor

Dr. Rebecca Lee Crumpler became the very first Black woman to become a doctor in the United States!

After working really hard, she earned her medical degree in Boston. But it wasn't easy because some people didn't think women or Black people should be doctors. But she didn't give up! She even went to Richmond, Virginia, to help people who had been enslaved during the Civil War. Dr. Crumpler was so kind and caring.

In 1883, she did something really cool – she wrote a special book called "A Book of Medical Discourses: In Two Parts." This book tells about her adventures as a doctor and how to take care of moms and kids. It's like a treasure chest of knowledge!

We can learn so much from Dr. Crumpler. She teaches us that we can achieve our dreams with hard work and determination no matter who we are or what we look like. She also shows us how important it is to be kind and help others, just like she did when she cared for people who needed it most.

To learn more about Dr. Rebecca Lee Crumpler, you can read her book, "A Book of Medical Discourses: In Two Parts," or "Dr. Rebecca Lee Crumpler: Doctress of Medicine" by Sheryl Recinos, about her life and her incredible journey. There are also websites and museums that tell her story.

Booker T. Washington
Wizard of Tuskegee

Booker Taliaferro Washington was an amazing person who lived long ago in the United States. He was born in 1856 and did many important things during his lifetime.

One of the most special things about Booker T. Washington was that he helped a lot of people learn and grow. He started a school called the Tuskegee Institute in Alabama, where he taught African-American students important skills like farming and craftsmanship. This was a big deal because, at that time, not all kids had the same opportunities to learn.

Booker T. Washington did some incredible things in his life. He became a famous speaker, which means he talked to lots of people and inspired them with his words. He even advised some of the important leaders of the United States!

We can learn a lot from Booker T. Washington. He showed us that no matter where we come from, we can achieve great things if we work hard and never give up. He believed in the power of education and wanted all kids to have a chance to learn and succeed.

If you want to know more about this amazing person, you can read his books, like "Up from Slavery" and "The Story of My Life and Work." His life is full of interesting stories that can teach us valuable lessons.

Garrett Morgan

Inventor of the Traffic Light and the Gas Mask

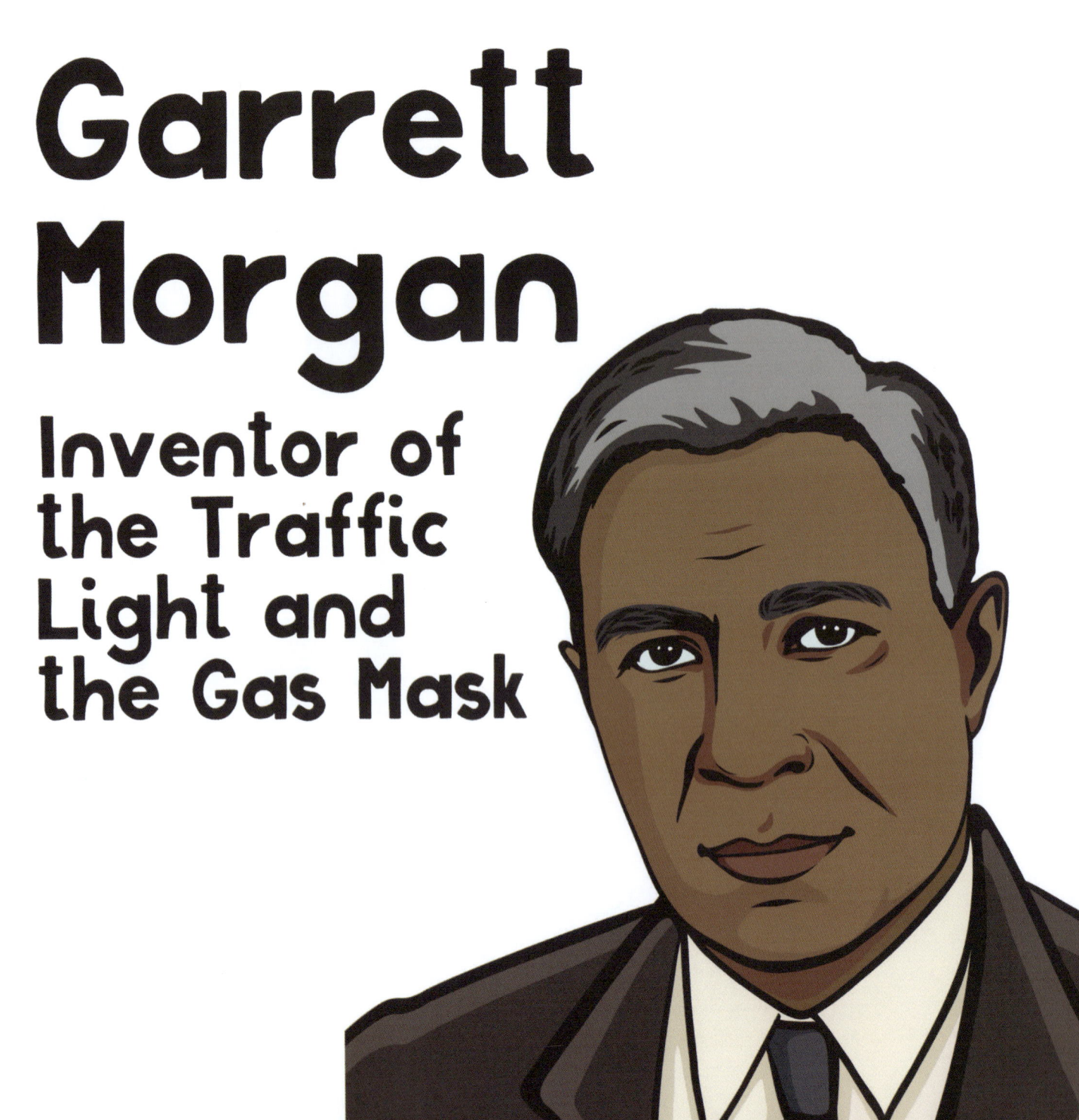

Let's travel back in time to meet a remarkable inventor named Garrett Morgan. He lived a long time ago, in the early 1900s, in the United States. But guess what? He did some really cool things that are still helping us today!

First, Garrett Morgan made our streets safer. You know those traffic lights with red, green, and yellow? Well, he's the genius who made them better! Before him, traffic lights were not as clear, and it was hard for drivers to know when to stop or go. Thanks to Garrett, we now have these colorful lights that keep our roads organized and safe.

But that's not all! He also invented something really important called the gas mask. Imagine a mask that helps you breathe safely, even in places with dangerous gases or smoke. Garrett Morgan created that! During a brave rescue mission, he used his gas mask to save lives from a big underground explosion. He was a true hero!

Garrett Morgan shows us that anyone can be a hero and make the world a better place, no matter where they come from or what they look like. He also reminds us to always think about safety. Whether it's on the road or in an emergency, we should be careful and think of ways to protect ourselves and help others. Garrett Morgan did just that, and we can do it too!

If you want to learn more about this awesome inventor, you can watch a short film about him titled "The Inventor: The Story of Garrett Morgan." So, let's keep exploring and be inspired by Garrett Morgan, the inventor who made the world safer and better!

Sister Rosetta Tharpe

The Godmother Of Rock 'N' Roll

Let's step into the world of music and meet a sensational lady named Sister Rosetta Tharpe. She lived in a time when colorful music was just starting to rock and roll! Rosetta was like a musical wizard, and her songs were pure magic.

Sister Rosetta Tharpe was no ordinary singer. She sang gospel music that made everyone feel joyful and alive. But she added something special – the sound of the electric guitar! Can you imagine? Back then, guitars weren't played like she did. She made it rock and roll!

She sang with so much energy and heart that people called her the "Godmother of Rock 'n' Roll." She played her guitar so cool that many famous rock stars later said she inspired them. She was a superstar, and her music made the world dance!

Sister Rosetta Tharpe showed us that music is a fantastic way to bring joy and happiness to people. She shared her love for music with the world, and it made a big difference. We can all spread happiness in our own way, just like she did! She proved that you can be amazing at something, even if it's not what everyone expects. She mixed gospel with rock and roll and created a brand-new sound. So, no matter what you love to do, you can make it special and unique, just like Sister Rosetta did with her music.

If you want to learn more about Sister Rosetta Tharpe, you can read books, like "Shout, Sister, Shout!: The Untold Story of Rock-and-Roll Trailblazer Sister Rosetta Tharpe," about her life and listen to her fantastic music!

Rosa Parks

The Mother of the Civil Rights Movement

Let's journey back to a time when buses were different. In 1955, in Montgomery, Alabama, there was a special lady named Rosa Parks. She did something very brave and important on a bus that changed the world!

One day, Rosa Parks got on a bus after a long day of work. But when the bus got crowded, the driver said she had to give up her seat just because of the color of her skin. Rosa said, "No, I won't!" She stayed in her seat and didn't move. This was a big deal because, back then, the rules were unfair. But Rosa was strong and stood up for what was right.

Her brave act inspired lots of people. They decided not to ride the buses until things changed. This was called the Montgomery Bus Boycott, and it was an important step in making the rules fairer for everyone.

Rosa Parks teaches us that even when things seem unfair, we can use our voices to make a difference. We can stand up for what's right, just like she did on that bus. She also reminds us that one person's courage can spark a big change. Rosa's bravery started a whole movement! So, no matter how small we might feel, we can make a big impact when we do what's right.

If you want to learn more about this amazing hero, you can read her book, "Rosa Parks: My Story," about her life and the civil rights movement. Rosa Parks' bravery is a shining light in history, and we can all be inspired by her!

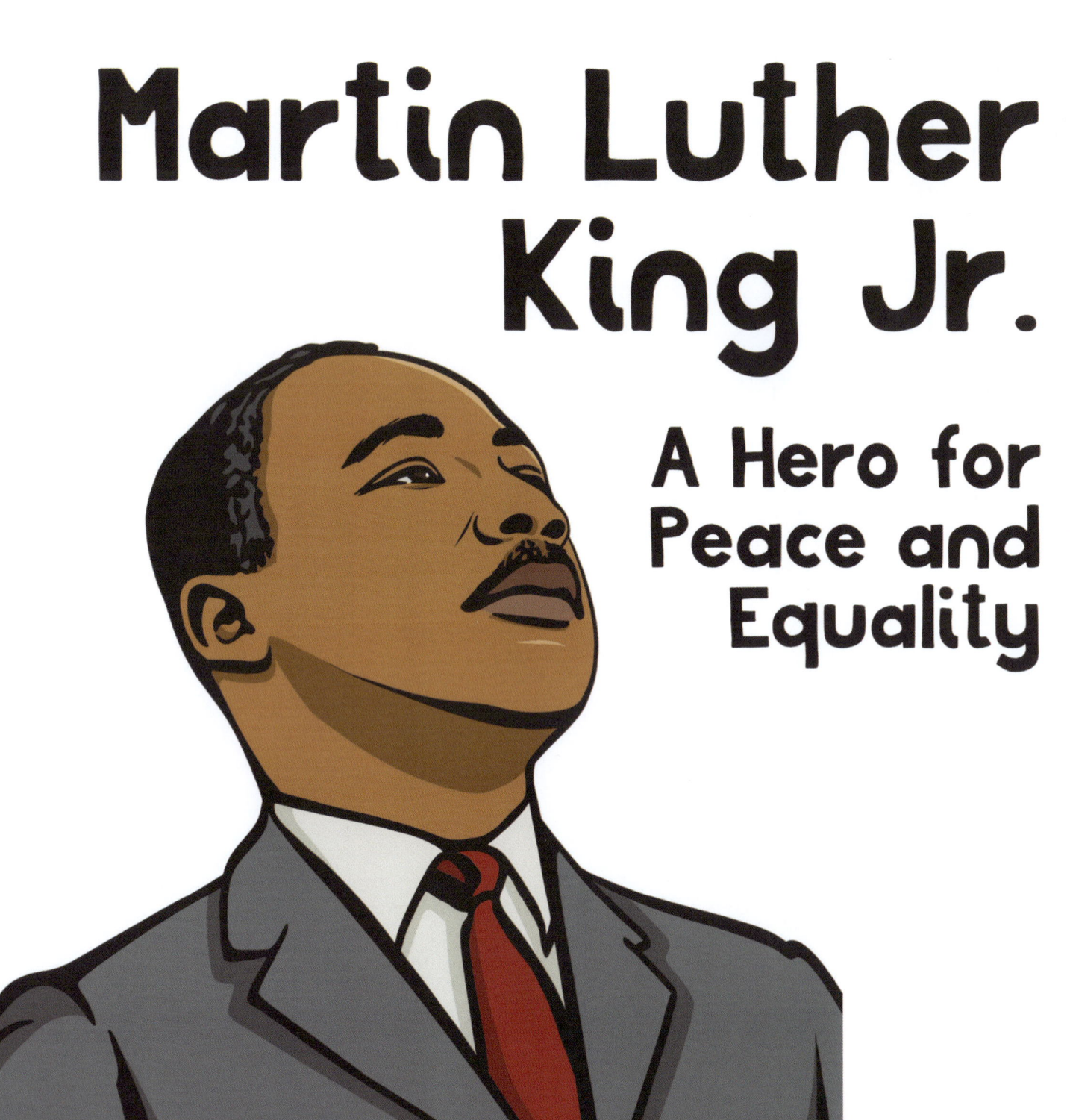

A long time ago, in America, there was a wonderful person named Martin Luther King Jr., who dreamed of a world where everyone was treated with kindness and fairness, no matter the color of their skin.

Martin had a big dream. He wanted everyone to live together in peace and harmony. He used his words, not fists, to make his dream come true. He gave a famous speech called "I Have a Dream" that made people believe in a better world.

He also worked really hard to change unfair laws. He wanted all children to go to the same schools and all people to sit together on buses. His kindness and bravery helped make America a more equal and fair place.

He teaches us that no dream is too big. If we work hard and believe in ourselves, we can make the world better, just like he did. He also showed us that kindness and love are stronger than hate. Even when faced with unfairness, he chose peace and love, and it made a big difference. We can all be like him and choose kindness in our lives.

To learn more about this incredible hero, you can read his public speech "I Have a Dream" and his book, like "A Time to Break Silence: The Essential Works of Martin Luther King, Jr., for Students." Martin Luther King Jr. left a legacy of love and equality, and we can be inspired by his words and actions!

Muhammad Ali
The Greatest

Once upon a time, in a world of boxing and bravery, there lived an amazing hero named Muhammad Ali. He was born in 1942 in Kentucky, USA. But he didn't just box in the ring; he also fought for important things outside it!

Muhammad Ali was like a superhero in the boxing ring. He was quick, strong, and super smart. He won the heavyweight boxing championship not once, not twice, but three times! People called him "The Greatest" because he truly was.

But Ali didn't just fight with his fists. He also used his voice for good. He stood up for what he believed in, like fairness and peace. Even when it was hard, he stayed true to his beliefs. He showed the world that we should all be treated the same, no matter where we come from or what we look like.

Muhammad Ali teaches us that we can be great at what we love if we work hard and believe in ourselves. He proved that with his boxing skills. He also reminds us to stand up for what's right, even when it's not easy. He fought for fairness and peace and used his voice to make the world a better place. We can all be like Ali and make a difference in our own way.

To learn more about this incredible champion, you can watch the movie "Ali" or read books about his life, like "The Greatest: My Own Story." Muhammad Ali's life is a story of courage, strength, and hope, and we can all be inspired by it!

In the exciting world of basketball, there was a man named Michael Jordan. He was born in 1963 in Brooklyn, New York. But he didn't just play basketball; he soared to incredible heights, and his story is like a fairy tale!

Michael Jordan was like a wizard with a basketball. He could jump really high and score points like magic! He played for a team called the Chicago Bulls and won not one, not two, but six NBA championships! People called him "Air Jordan" because he could fly in the air when he dunked the basketball.

But it wasn't just about winning games for Michael; he showed us that hard work and never giving up are the real keys to success. He didn't make his high school basketball team at first, but he practiced and practiced until he became the best!

Michael Jordan shows us that even if we face challenges, like not making a team, we can keep trying and get better. He never gave up, and that's why he became a superstar. He also reminds us that being a team player is important. Even though he was the best, he always helped his teammates and made them better, too. We can all be like Michael by working hard and being good teammates in our own games and adventures!

To learn more about this incredible basketball legend, you can watch "Michael Jordan: Above & Beyond (1996)" or watch videos of his amazing basketball moves on YouTube. Michael Jordan's journey is an inspiration to dream big and work hard to reach for the stars!

Eldrick Tont Woods

Tiger

In the wonderful world of golf, there was a magical golfer named Tiger Woods. He was born in 1975 in California, USA, and he played golf like a champ!

Tiger Woods was a golf expert. He won so many important golf tournaments that it's hard to count! He even won something called the "Masters Tournament" lots of times. His nickname was given to him by his father in honor of his close friend in the army, Colonel Vuong Dang Phong, who was also referred to as "Tiger." But people loved to call him "Tiger" because he was fierce and strong, like a tiger in the golf course jungle.

But it wasn't just about winning for Tiger. He taught us that if we practice and work really hard, we can achieve our dreams. He started playing golf when he was just a little kid, and he kept getting better and better.

Tiger Woods teaches us that practice and determination can make us great at something we love. Whether it's golf, painting, or playing an instrument, we can be amazing with hard work. He also reminds us that even when things get tough, we can bounce back. Tiger had some challenges in his golf journey, but he never gave up. We can be like him, staying strong and facing our challenges head-on.

To learn more about this incredible golfer, you can read books, like "Tiger Woods" by Armen Keteyian and Jeff Benedict, or watch videos of his amazing golf shots. Tiger Woods is an inspiration for anyone who dreams big and loves to play!

Barack Obama

A History-Making Leader

Once upon a time, in America, there was a special person named Barack Obama. He became the leader of the country in the year 2009, and he lived in a big, white house called the White House.

Barack Obama did many amazing things during his time as a leader. He signed important laws that helped people have better healthcare and even made it possible for more kids to attend school. One of the coolest things about him is that he became the very first African-American to be the boss of the whole country!

We can learn from Barack Obama that we can achieve big dreams no matter where we come from or what we look like. He taught us to be kind to each other and to help those who need it. He believed that everyone deserves a chance to be their best, and that's something we can all strive for.

If you want to learn even more about Barack Obama, you can read books like "Barack Obama: The Story" by David Maraniss or his books, "A Promised Land" or "Dreams from My Father." His story is full of inspiration for kids just like you!

Remember, Barack Obama showed us that anyone can make history and make the world a better place. So, dream big and be kind, just like this remarkable leader did!

Whitney Houston

The Voice

In a land of music and melodies, there lived a singing superstar named Whitney Houston. She was born in Newark, USA, and her voice was like pure magic.

Whitney Houston sang songs that touched our hearts. She sang about love, friendship, and believing in ourselves. Whitney won many awards and became known as "The Voice," one of the greatest singers ever. You might have heard her famous song "I Will Always Love You" - it's a song that makes people feel happy inside.

From Whitney, we can learn that our dreams can come true if we practice and never give up. Her songs remind us to be kind to others and spread love. Whitney inspired many people with her music, showing us that we can use our talents to make the world a better place.

If you want to learn more about Whitney, you can read the book written by her close friend, Robyn Crawford, "A Song for You: My Life with Whitney Houston."
 If you want to hear Whitney Houston's beautiful songs and see her smile, you can ask grown-ups to play her music. Her music and story will fill your heart with happiness!

Whitney Houston was a gift to the world. She taught us to believe in ourselves and share our talents. So, sing your heart out, be kind, and spread love, just like "the Voice" did!

Maya Angelou
A Magical Storyteller

Maya Angelou was an incredible person who lived in America not too long ago. She was born in 1928 and did so many amazing things in her life.

Maya Angelou was a wonderful writer and poet. She wrote beautiful books and poems that made people think and feel. One of her most famous books is "I Know Why the Caged Bird Sings." It's a story about her own life and the challenges she faced.

She also stood up for what she believed in. She was a civil rights activist, which means she worked hard to make sure everyone was treated fairly, regardless of skin color. Her words and actions inspired many people to do the same.

Maya Angelou taught us that words are powerful. Through her writing and speeches, she showed us how words can change the world. She also taught us to be brave and speak up when we see something that's not right. Maya's life story reminds us that even when we face tough times, we can still grow and become amazing people.

To learn more about Maya Angelou, you can read books and poems she wrote, like "I Know Why the Caged Bird Sings" or "And Still I Rise." You can also find videos of her speaking and sharing her wisdom.

Maya Angelou's life is a beautiful example of how one person can make a big difference in the world.

That's all for now!

We hope you and your children enjoyed reading this book.

If you did, we'd really appreciate you leaving a review on Amazon.

Thank you for reading.

We wish you the best of luck in your own journey to becoming a Black Icon!

New books coming soon!

Please follow our Author Page on Amazon to stay up to date with future releases!

Printed in Great Britain
by Amazon